MW00617412

Bowing To Yoga?

The truth about the roots and fruits of yoga

Armin Weidle

RSI
PUBLISHING

Raising the Standard Publishing LLC

For the sake of better readability of this book, the male substantive form is being used throughout the book. Of course, it includes the female form in terms of content.

i

Books may be ordered through booksellers or by
contacting:

Armin Weidle
bowing2yoga@gmail.com
https://www.facebook.com/bowing2yoga/
Frankfurt, Germany

Published by RSIP
Raising the Standard International Publishing L. L. C.
https://www.rsiministry.com
Navarre, Florida

ISBN: 9781955830461

Printed in Germany
2nd Edition Date: January 2022

Contents

Foreword

In the previous fifty years the Western world has turned increasingly away from faith in the concept of objective knowledge. Scientific thought and its philosophical counterpart of scientism and rationalism reached its apex in the heyday of modernism. The catastrophes of World War Two and the gradual collapse of modernist faith in science have led to a remarkable resurgence of what can be described as transcendental mysticism. This resurgent philosophy was never fully absent in Western thought but has now come to dominate at least the leisure time of a significant portion of the Western world's population. Sometimes it is dressed up as "science" to make it palatable to a still scientifically oriented West. Other times it masquerades as a system for relaxation complete with studies showing its power to lower everything from cholesterol to blood pressure to body fat. One significant question needs to be asked: Does what we meditate on become who we are? Will the emphasis on personal transcendent experience ultimately trump faith in a rational, predictable, and manipulatable universe?

Armin Weidle's book, Bowing to Yoga, attempts to discern the roots of yoga and demonstrates the dangers of blithe acceptance of these "harmless" exercises. It is part of the hubris of the Western mind to believe all things can be de-contextualized and neutralized as to potential negative effects. Western philosophers as late as the 1970's wrote that India had never produced any philosophy of significance. Rubbish! The philosophy of yoga combined physical exercises with a remarkably subtle philosophy of mind at a time when most western Europeans were still cannibals. Weidle delves into these sophisticated roots, pointing out that India discerned more than 2000 years ago that highly unusual states of mind could be generated by careful body manipulation. I have personally witnessed that these states of mind can sometimes lead to psychosis.

Weidle's book is a helpful warning to the reader that there is far more to yoga than just exercises. In the issue of form and meaning, clearly this is a form that generates automatically, through breath control and body posture, significant changes in hormones, electrolytes, and the nervous system. These forms will create a certain state of mind, a certain meaning. This coupled, as Weidle points out, with the emptying of the mind of thought, creates an attitude amenable to change through experience. To put it another way, we become what we do. While it is possible that some may be able to maintain a purely distant, objective view of their experience, meditative consciousness is a powerful drug. Many have described it as more powerful than hallucinogens. There is always the danger of being drawn deeper into the experience. Weidle discerns how this ananda (joy) is defined as the divine within the self. As such, idolatry and self-worship, the hallmarks of Western self-preoccupation, are accepted as normative. It is ironic that the West is drifting to this wasteland of mindless experience at the same time that the East, China and India, is rapidly accepting the presuppositions of the modernist western world. Can anyone doubt that they will soon pass us economically, politically, and militarily?

Weidle correctly points out the seductiveness and destructiveness of this philosophy. This is a book well worth reading, digesting, and reacting to. I highly recommend it to thoughtful readers.

Dr. David Cashin
Professor of Intercultural Studies
Columbia International University
Columbia, South Carolina

Acknowledgments

A project about the roots and fruits of yoga has been on my heart for a long time. I am grateful that with much help and encouragement from the Lord Jesus and great friends, it has become a reality.

First, I want to thank my Lord Jesus for leading me to write this book. Without the inspiration through the Holy Spirit this book would not have become a reality. Second, I want to thank my wife Ratna for all her support and valuable insights, which helped me finish this book well. Third, I want I want to thank my parents for their support and help that freed me up to write this book. Fourth, I want to thank Eric and Kristi Bothur for their help with editing. This book is more readable because of the hard work that you put into the editing process. I also want to thank my former professor, Dr. David Cashin, for his cultural insight and encouragement to publish this book.

Thank you, Tom Spainhour, for giving input on how to improve the content of my manuscript and giving me new ideas. Thank you, Paul Kaufmann, for reading my manuscript and for your valuable insights. Thank you, Christopher Witdoeckt, for asking great questions to help me set goals and challenging me to re-think what I wrote. Thank you,

Laurette Willis, for your help in the section "Alternatives to Yoga" and for sharing your testimony. Thank you, Tara, for sharing your testimony. May it be an encouragement to many. Thank you, Lynnette Spokes, for your help with finding good web resources. Richard Cheng provided great help with the illustrations in the appendix -- thank you. Finally, I want to thank Jialiang Wu for all his input about spiritual warfare. I learned a lot from you.

Armin Weidle

Introduction

Today, yoga is widely practiced in North America and Europe, and it is becoming more and more popular as an alternative to exercises like running, swimming, biking, or going to the gym. In the U.S. alone, there are about 16 million people who practice some kind of yoga and the numbers of those who try yoga for the first time are constantly growing. Yoga often stands out from other exercises because of its holistic approach, as it engages body, soul, and mind. Fans of yoga praise it for its effectiveness in helping a person relax, reduce stress, loosen muscle tension, lose weight, and even strengthen the immune system. Yoga definitely does have physical benefits, but there are also dangers involved in practicing it, dangers that stem from its roots. Many people who practice yoga in the West do not know what it really is and what its true roots and fruits are, nor do they know about the possible dangers of it. Yoga instructors generally do not inform practitioners, particularly those looking for physical benefits and stress reduction, of yoga's background or possible dangers.

In recent years, yoga has also been the topic of much discussion and several kinds of literature have been written about it. First, there is literature that promotes yoga, written by authors who present yoga mostly from a Hindu perspective. Second, there is Christian literature that examines yoga in light of the Bible, and third, there are authors who present a so-called "Christian Yoga", which basically means to implement yoga in a Christian context. This book will mention opinions of authors from all three categories to show how yoga is being discussed. To present some of those views about yoga does not mean that I believe they show the full picture of yoga or that I agree with everything these authors mention, but they will show different perspectives on yoga. My purpose in writing this book is to provide information on what has not been discussed much in publications so far, to show the truth about the roots and fruits of yoga, and to raise awareness of the dangers inherent in it.

To explain the origins of yoga, this book includes many Hindu terms with which you may be unfamiliar. To aid in understanding the information about yoga, you will find an explanation of these terms in the glossary at the end of the book.

PART ONE

Origin and Foundations of Yoga

Armin Weidle

Chapter One

The Roots of Yoga

Yoga is based on a written text called the *Yoga Sutras*, which were written by a Hindu guru named Patanjali between A.D. 300 and 500. However, its roots go back much further to about 3000 B.C. It originated in India and is a part of the six major philosophical/religious systems in Hinduism.

The basic goal of yoga is unification of the self (*atman*) with the supreme reality (*Brahman*). This is already indicated in the word yoga itself, as it is derived from the root word *yuj*, which means "to yoke" or "to unite." Yoga attempts to unite body, spirit, and mind in a harmonious whole through various breathing exercises (*pranayama*), physical postures (*asanas*) and meditation, with the goal of realizing the divine within self. To understand more about the roots of yoga, let us look at its foundational elements, which include the four major paths of yoga and the eight parts of yoga (also called limbs).

The four major paths of yoga are as follows:

1. *Raja Yoga* is the science of physical and mental control and focuses on methods to control

thoughts by turning mental and physical energy into spiritual energy.

2. *Jnana Yoga* emphasizes knowledge and wisdom; through strength of will and intellect, the yogi attempts to remove the barriers to his unity with the spirit world.

3. *Karma Yoga* is action oriented and emphasizes the purification of the heart to act selflessly and to detach oneself from thinking about the fruits of one's actions.

4. *Bhakti Yoga* focuses on devotion and emphasizes surrender to a so-called supreme cosmic spirit through prayer, worship and ritual, channeling, and transmuting emotions into unconditional love or devotion.

Central to the system of yoga are the eight limbs (parts) that are defined by Patanjali as:[2]

1. *Yama:* self control, restraint, devotion to the gods or to the supreme reality (*Brahman*).

2. *Niyama:* religious duties, prohibitions, observances.

3. *Asanas:* physical postures for yoga practices.

4. *Pranayama:* the control and directing of the

6

breath and the divine energy within the human body to promote health and spiritual consciousness.

5. *Pratyahara:* sensory control or deprivation, i.e., withdrawal of senses from attachment to external objects.

6. *Dharana:* deeper concentration, or mind control.

7. *Dhyana:* deep contemplation.

8. *Samadhi:* highest state of mental concentration where enlightenment or *Brahman* realization, i.e. union of the individual with the divine, is supposed to take place.

In his attempt to define yoga, Buddhist scholar Robert Thurman explains that according to Patanjali, "Yoga is the actuality of our union with the absolute, the supreme reality of ourselves... the blissful void, freedom, or what is called Absolute Glory (*Brahman, nirvana*), god (*Ishvar*), or Buddha, Reality Embodied (*Dharmakaya*), and many other names."[3]

Louis Hughes, a yoga practitioner and author in Ireland, in his book *Yoga - A Path to God?* lists four definitions of yoga. Hughes says that according to the *Katha Upanishad,* written in the fifth century B.C., yoga is described as the steady holding of the senses. He goes on to explain that according to the *Yoga Sutras,* yoga is the restraint of the processes of the mind, and he says that the *Bhagavad-Gita* (Hindu scripture) describes yoga as mystical discipline with the goal of uniting the human and divine soul. Lastly, he states that according to India's national epic poem the *Mahabharata,* yoga is seen as practical discipline or activity that leads the soul to *Brahman*.[4] In Hindu philosophy, this is portrayed as a person's soul being united with the ocean of the divine (described as supreme reality), like a drop of water that is united with the ocean.

Chapter Two

The Yoga of the West

Yoga first came to America in 1893 through a Hindu Guru named Swami Vivekanda and was more widely spread through Swami Yogananda in the 1920's. According to a poll by Yoga Journal/Harris Interactive in 2008, 15.8 million people (6.9 % of U.S. adults) practiced yoga in the U.S., with 72.2 % of yoga practitioners being women. This poll also showed that 18.3 million people who do not practice yoga currently, said that they are very interested in yoga (this is triple the number of a 2004 study). Also 9.3 million non-practitioners said that they would try yoga within the next year.[5] These numbers show that yoga is popular in the U.S and that interest in yoga is growing. Not only is yoga popular in the U.S., but there is also a growing interest in Europe. In the 1930's, a few decades after it had reached America, yoga came to Europe in the form of Hatha Yoga and the classical yoga by Patanjali (eight limbs). The yoga by Patanjali differs from Hatha Yoga in that it uses mostly sitting meditation postures aiming to lead a person to liberation, whereas Hatha Yoga employs various physical postures, which are designed to purify the body and mind.

Yoga is practiced in different forms around the world today. The form of yoga that is most popular in the U.S. and Europe is Hatha Yoga with its focus on physical postures and breathing techniques. The original purpose of Hatha Yoga according to *Vendantic* philosophy is to experience the oneness of all existence. Swami Vishnu Devananda, founder of the Yoga Center in San Francisco, states that Hatha Yoga is adapted to the needs of modern men through relaxation, breathing, exercise, diet, and right thinking.[6]

Kundalini Yoga (yoga of awareness), which adds the additional elements of chanting and meditation, is another form of yoga that is finding more and more acceptance in the West. Kundalini Yoga assumes the existence of "serpent power", energy located at the base of the spine that can be awakened and utilized through yoga. The purpose of Kundalini Yoga is to utilize this power and direct it to the brain. Seminars and workshops are offered at yoga institutions, health institutions, schools, and even at some churches. Some of them even offer yoga for children. There are yoga centers all over the U.S. and Europe where people retreat to learn to eliminate the distractions of life with the goal of getting in touch with their true self. See Table 1 for a basic comparison of these two popular forms of yoga.

Two popular forms of yoga in the Western World

Table 1 is a brief summary of Hatha Yoga and Kundalini Yoga.

	Hatha Yoga	Kundalini Yoga
Focus	Physical postures, breathing	Meditation and chanting
Purpose	Relaxation, stress reduction, improvement of health leading to oneness with universe	Seeks to strengthen the inner self and bring awareness of it
Method	Physical postures in various shapes (e.g. sun, tree, corpse) and also meditative breathing exercises	Release of energy at spine (serpent power) through meditation and chanting

Table 1

Most popular forms of Hatha Yoga

Hatha Yoga comes in a number of different forms. Here is a brief introduction to the most common ones. Any of the different types of yoga below, is still considered Hatha Yoga.[7]

11

Iyengar is often used as the beginner yoga. It focuses on aligning the body to help students who lack flexibility. It is used for physical therapy because of its focus on the movement of the joints.

Kripalu is sometimes called the yoga of consciousness. It teaches students to pay attention to their physical and psychological reactions to different postures. Three stages are involved: learning the postures, holding the postures, and combining them into a kind of meditation in motion.

Viniyoga is the most highly customized form of yoga. The stretching postures are adjusted to each student's needs and abilities. The function of a posture is emphasized over its form, with a focus on integrating the flow of breath with the movement of the spine.

Sivananda is the rigorous application of yoga postures, breathing exercises, relaxation, and vegetarian diet. It also involves the study of Hindu scriptures.

Ashtanga is also known as Power Yoga. Students jump from one posture to another to build strength, stamina, and flexibility, while practicing breath control at the same time.

Jivamukti is a variation of Ashtanga with a

focus on spiritual training that includes chanting, meditation, and readings.

Bikram or Choudhury is also known as Hot Yoga. With a surrounding temperature of 100°F (38°C) or more, the yoga instructor leads the students through 26 postures that are designed to stretch muscles and tendons in a specific order. The heat warms the muscles, and enables them to stretch farther.

Armin Weidle

PART TWO

The Fruits of Yoga

Armin Weidle

Chapter Three

Is Yoga More Than Exercise?

Have you ever thought about what the fruits of yoga are? We have discussed the physical benefits, but what about the spiritual side of yoga? Could there be any dangers in practicing yoga? In the West, yoga, especially Hatha Yoga, is often presented as physical yoga and many people practice it to exercise and to experience stress relief. Usually, they do not want to engage in Hinduism, nor empty themselves to seek the divine within. Often, they think that they are just doing the postures (*asanas*), but very few people ask about the spiritual implications of the *asanas*, or even know that they exist. If the *asanas* were just physical in nature without any spiritual element, Hatha Yoga could be practiced just as any other exercise. Also, if the physical aspect of the *asanas* could be completely removed from their spiritual nature, there would be little concern with practicing Hatha Yoga as an exercise. The real question is whether anyone can practice Hatha Yoga without being affected by Hindu philosophy. If Hatha Yoga is not only a physical exercise, but an extension

17

of Hinduism, a person who practices it enters automatically into the spiritual realm of Hinduism even when that might not be visible at first.

Hatha Yoga is often described as yoga that prepares the body for the spiritual path via physical and breathing exercises. It prepares and conditions the body so that the mind can practice meditation without obstacles. Let us take a closer look at the *asanas*. Are they just physical postures or are they more than that? In this respect it is important to know that "yoga teaches that each posture reflects a mental attitude, whether that attitude be one of surrender, as in a forward bending *asana*, or the strengthening of the will, through backward bending postures, or the creation of a physical prayer or meditation with the body, as in the practice of the lotus posture."[8] In the visual arts of India, the word *asana* refers to the posture of a seated deity, a figure, or to the seat or throne on which he sits. By doing the yoga postures a person expresses meaning, which is spiritual in nature and is of Hindu origin. Let us now consider what several yoga experts have to say about the spiritual effects of Hatha Yoga.

Hindu scholar and author Ravi Ravindra emphasizes that although there are many kinds of yoga, the Indian tradition has in general maintained that there is only one central yoga, with the one aim of harnessing the entire body and mind to the purposes of the supreme reality (*Brahman*).[9] He further says that the ground to be prepared is the entire psychosomatic organism, for it is through that

that *purusa* (true understanding) and *prajna* (transcendental insight) arise.[10] This demonstrates that the intention is for yoga to not solely stay in the physical realm, but to affect the whole being of a person (body, mind, soul, and spirit).

Professor of Hinduism at the Monastic Institute of Interreligious Dialogue in San'Anselmo, Italy, Thomas Matus confirms that yoga is more than exercise and states, "Even those who limit their contact with it to a few hours each week at the gymnasium or health facility cannot avoid the spiritual implications of doing yoga."[11] Matus' statement makes clear that one does not even need to spend much time practicing yoga in order to be affected spiritually.

German author Jakob Wilhelm Hauer states that genuine yoga always starts from the core of the inner being. Quoting *Yoga Sutra* II, 47, Hauer says that even the lowest form of yoga that is practiced in Hatha Yoga, with the postures and physical exercises, has not only a body and soul aspect, but also an inner-metaphysical one. The breathing exercises are seen as a tool to reach inner enlightenment. These along with pondering, prepare the senses to be drawn into the next stage. This next stage is the complete abstraction when the senses are removed from everything external and become one with the internal (*YS* II, 54),[12] which means that the senses do not notice outside things anymore, but are completely focused on the internal with the goal to discover the inner self of a person. According to Hinduism, the inner self of a person is divine. Hinduism also explains that if distractions to focusing on the internal are removed well enough, the person will realize over time that he is divine. Hatha Yoga has the same purpose, to get a person to focus inwardly, to focus on self, and to withdraw from anything outward.

Brad Scott, a Christian author who comments on Hatha Yoga, writes in an article for *The Watchman Expositor* that "to practice Hatha Yoga is to accept the doctrine of Raja Yoga, involving the coiled serpent-power at the base of the spine (*kundalini*), seven *chakras* [seven main centers of energy in the human body], postures (*asanas*), and meditation (*dharana* and *dhyana*)."[13] Raja Yoga is one of the four major paths in Hinduism to attain liberation from the cycle of rebirth (*moksha*) and is in its thrust deeply spiritual. Hatha Yoga developed from Raja Yoga and can therefore be considered a branch of it. This also means that Raja Yoga instilled its spiritual nature into Hatha Yoga and therefore the underlying purpose of experiencing unification with the inner self, described as *samadhi*, is the same in Hatha Yoga as in Raja Yoga.

Johanna Michaelsen, a Christian writer on occult practices who lives in California, also makes it very clear that Hatha Yoga is more than exercise. She says, "There is a common misconception in the West that Hatha Yoga, one of the about ten forms of yoga that supposedly leads to self realization, is merely a neutral form of exercise, a soothing and effective alternative for those who abhor jogging and calisthenics . . . . [However], Hatha Yoga is one of the six recognized systems of orthodox Hinduism and is at its roots religious and mystical."[14]

Author Irving Hexham says about people who practice yoga for the purpose of exercise or stress relief, "As time passes, such people very gradually and imperceptibly begin to accept other concepts which involve definite religious convictions."[15] Even though they might not have had any intention in the beginning to seek the spiritual through yoga, it is likely that gradually their spiritual beliefs are being changed through their yoga practice. Diane Barnes, yoga instructor at "Mind-Body-Health" as well as at the University of South Carolina and Columbia College, all in Columbia, South Carolina, states that the real purpose of Hatha Yoga is to help people go deeper than only the physical postures. It appears that Hatha Yoga is more than exercise and is also designed to have spiritual influence on people who practice it. Two women who were involved in yoga confirm this.

Laurette Willis from Oklahoma tells the following about her experience concerning yoga. "I'd been involved in yoga, metaphysics and the New Age movement since the age of seven when my mother became interested in yoga," Laurette says. As her mother grew in her interest in yoga and started to teach free yoga classes in her home, she used her daughter as a model to demonstrate the postures. Gradually her mother's life ended in depression and suicide in 1982, which Laurette ascribes in part to her increased involvement in yoga keeping her from living a victorious Christian life. For Laurette this initial encounter with yoga also opened up the door to a New Age lifestyle that led her down a destructive path and kept her from knowing the true God for many years. "For the next twenty-two years I was heavily involved in many aspects of the New Age -- Yoga, Universal Mind, crystals, channelling, *Kabbala*, you-name-it. I was an alcoholic, compulsive overeater, I smoked and had a promiscuous, lonely lifestyle," she says. It was 1987 when Laurette began to question if what she had been believing about God was true. She surrendered her life to Jesus and started to experience freedom from these destructive habits. Today Laurette is a strong Christian and leads a ministry called PraiseMoves®, a Christian alternative to yoga. More about PraiseMoves® is provided in the chapter on alternatives to yoga.

Tara from Georgia (last name not mentioned to protect confidentiality) also has an interesting story to tell about her experience with yoga.[16]

Back in 2000 I started with a few classes in yoga and meditation, read some books on the topic, and started getting involved with Vedic astrology and the New Age. My goals for doing yoga ranged from weight loss to getting in touch with my inner self, yet when I look back I can say that yoga opened the door to a dark, spiraling road. When I think back on the appeal of yoga, I can't help thinking about all the promises and claims it makes to reel people in. Who does not want spiritual enlightenment, weight loss, and of course a longer life? It all looked so wonderful.

Bowing to Yoga

On one particular occasion when I was meditating to a CD on the Vedas, I focused my mind deeply on each one. The next thing I knew was this terrible sense of doom. I stopped! It boggled my mind that it did not evoke any serenity or peace, but I was getting the absolute opposite effect! "How could this be?" I thought to myself. I still didn't associate yoga, Hinduism, astrology and meditation with those experiences, so I continued. As I continued, terrible out-of-body experiences were somehow provoked. It started happening every night. I felt as if a heavy weight was over my entire body holding me down. I felt horrible fear and terror as I fought whatever this force was. Though I did not consider myself a Christian, I prayed to Jesus to make it stop, and He always did!

I finally quit yoga after those initial classes, but during a trip to India in 2003, I began doing it again. This time my primary goal was weight loss. I would meet a woman in her home every morning for my lessons. She would teach me yogic breathing, and various postures. I remember sitting on the floor, chanting "ommmm" and a sense of weakness and helplessness coming over me. Instead of the peace and serenity that others praised yoga for, I felt weak, vulnerable, powerless, and as if I was losing control.

Over time, during my time in India, the out-of-body attacks became so strong that I was literally afraid to go to sleep. Sometimes I would wake up in a pool of sweat, screaming, because I was so frightened. This continued to happen every night so I finally quit the yoga class and things improved slightly until I sought some help from a Vedic astrologer. After that, I ended up spiraling down in terrible illnesses and my life was being consumed by demonic energies. In the midst of it, though, I denied that the religion I was following could be responsible.

After I returned to the U.S.A., things reached an all-time low for me. I became suicidal, depressed, and horribly confused. So I sought help from my Vedic astrologer again, who suggested that I avoid certain things, wear charms, and do strange black magic rituals. My situation did not improve at all, though, until one night, I felt this voice speaking to me to go to a nearby church for a prayer meeting. When I went to the church I hesitated to go in, because I didn't want to change my religion, I didn't want to be told that Jesus was the only way to freedom, and I didn't want my beloved astrology removed from me. A man saw me standing outside the church and asked if he could help me. I said, "Yeah, is this where you have prayer meetings?" The man said "yes", and asked me if I was a Christian. My answer was pretty vague. I said, "I believe there is more than one way to truth." At this point, I didn't feel like hearing anything different. The man kept talking to me, though, quoting the Bible, and a light started to shine all around him. I felt so peaceful and thought I could trust what he was saying, so I kept listening.

That night I accepted Jesus Christ as Lord of my life. I turned back from my involvement with yoga, astrology, and Hinduism and I threw all my books in the garbage. For the first time I slept soundly, full of love and peace. I was free in Christ! The miserable demonic attacks stopped completely, and each day was full of joy, and not confusion.

After I moved to another state, I went through a very stressful time, and I began doing astrology and yoga again. Twenty-four hours after doing the yoga exercises, I came close to a nervous breakdown. I was depressed and *overcome by suicidal thoughts. I knew immediately that it was a demonic attack. I repented and had Christian friends pray for me and was delivered again. Jesus was faithful and forgave me.*

Today I am totally free in Christ and will never practice yoga again. I am convinced that no matter how the truth is sugar-coated, the fact remains that yoga is a dangerous time bomb ready to explode in your life at any time. It can and it will spiritually harm you. Today, the lies and distortions of Hindu ideas and yoga have found their way into many Christian churches, and Christians are slowly being deceived by the devil.

These sources clearly answer the question of whether yoga, specifically the popular Hatha Yoga, is more than exercise. Hatha Yoga is not merely designed as a physical exercise, but with definite intentions to influence people spiritually. The postures (*asanas*) convey spiritual (Hindu) meaning and they are designed to draw people into the realm of Hinduism. No matter what form of yoga, this underlying purpose stays the same. In this respect one must remember that the spiritual influence of yoga will always come straight from its origin, which is based in Hinduism. Therefore, there is a possibility that a person who practices yoga will over time integrate values from Hinduism into his life. Even though a person might not practice yoga with the intention to seek the spiritual in the first place, he still needs to realize that just doing yoga postures like the Corpse Pose, the Lotus Position, or the Cobra Pose, expresses Hindu meaning, whether knowingly or unknowingly. It is important to realize that because the *asanas* are designed to convey Hindu beliefs and principles, there is a good chance that over time he will not only see yoga as an exercise, but also open himself to its spiritual meaning and begin to act upon it.

Chapter Four

Yoga and the Mind

In our search to discover the truth about the fruits of yoga, it is also very important to look at how yoga affects the mind of a person. All human actions start in the mind. We think of doing something first before we act upon it. We have ideas before they turn into reality. Therefore, it is crucial to guard our minds from negative influences so we will not take negative actions.

Satan's main target is the mind. If he is able to get a person to even think about his evil suggestions and furthermore agree with them, the person will move closer to acting upon them and will move away from what God wants him to do. In Genesis 3:1 Satan questions the Word of God with the goal of making Eve question it as well, saying, "Did God really say, 'You must not eat from any tree in the garden'?" Satan's attempt to manipulate Eve's mind goes on as he tells her, "You will not surely die" (Gen. 3:4). This form of mind manipulation was the trigger for Eve to turn away from God and attempt to find her satisfaction in something other than Him.

Because of this link between our thoughts and our actions we need to look at how yoga affects the mind of a person. The system of yoga declares that the body and mind are essentially one. This is in contrast to the biblical view where body and mind are seen as two separate entities that are connected to each other and dependent on each other. The intrinsic goal of yoga philosophy, to achieve complete unity of body and mind, is not how God created it to be. By its very nature, yoga is designed to go beyond the physical level to the spiritual and mental level in order to achieve complete unity of body and mind through the removal of any outward distractions. Although at first yoga influences the body, it does not stay on the physical level, but it will ultimately influence the mental level and transform the mind of a person as well. Christian researchers Dr. Ankerberg and Dr. Weldon confirm this, stating, "In yoga theory, the body is really a crude layer of one's mind, and both are aspects of the continuum of alleged divine consciousness that is 'awakened' by yoga practice. Therefore, manipulation of the body is equivalent to manipulation of the mind and spirit. This is why physical postures of yoga are designed to manipulate consciousness toward a specific occult goal."[17]

Yoga proposes that a person can find his true self and a unification of body, soul, and mind by "emptying" his mind. To empty one's mind means to remove any outward distractions through the practice of yoga by focusing inwardly. This is mostly done through a combination of yoga postures and meditation. At first glance, to empty one's mind seems harmless, yet it is important to find out if there could be any dangers to it. In order to do that, it is helpful to look at the processes of the brain and find out if the practice of yoga can lead to an altered state of mind. Sir John Carew Eccles of Australia, a 1963 Nobel prize winner in physiology/medicine and an expert on the human brain, has stated,

> The brain is "a machine that a ghost can operate." In a normal state of consciousness, one's own spirit ticks off the neurons in his brain and operates his body. We are spirits connected with a body. But in an altered state, reached under drugs, yoga, hypnosis etc., this passive but alert state, the connection between the spirit and the brain, is loosened. This allows another spirit to interpose itself, to begin to tick off the neurons in the brain and create an entire universe of illusion.[18]

Eccles' discoveries about the human brain clearly show that it can reach an altered state through yoga, which can open up a person to the influence of dangerous spirits. A person might try to find god by practicing yoga and emptying his mind, but in reality it is possible that he is opening himself up to the influence of evil. People who enter deeper into yoga, especially into the spiritual realm, should be aware of those dangers.

Another example of how yoga can affect the mind of a human being can been seen in the research of Donald J. DeGracia, Ph.D. DeGracia is a professor at the Center for Molecular Medicine and Genetics at Wayne State University in Detroit, Michigan. He has researched the question of whether psychotropic drugs mimic the awakened *kundalini* (serpent power at the spine) and has found out that most of the effects are identical. For example, some of the effects in both cases are a trembling of the body, sensations of hot or cold, sensory and audio hallucinations, extreme feelings of fear, and loss or dissociation of emotions.[19] The similarities between the altered state of consciousness in yoga and the one caused by psychotropic drugs are striking, and it is clear that the effects on the mind and on the whole person in each case are negative.

These sources show that yoga can have an impact on the mind that can be oppressive and destructive. In the Bible we see that God has not given us a spirit of fear, but of power and of love and of a sound mind (2 Tim. 1:7). It becomes clear that the methods in yoga to manipulate the mind towards "thinking Hinduism" are counterproductive to the knowledge of the personal God of the Bible. God describes Himself as not being the author of confusion but of peace (1 Cor. 14:33). The possible effects of yoga, as mentioned before, are certainly not a mark of His influence on a human being.

Chapter Five

Yoga -- God Within Self?

Since the often-stated purpose of yoga is union with the divine, we must ask what "union with the divine" means and how "the divine" is portrayed. "Union with the divine" as it is seen within the system of yoga does not mean a personal relationship with God, but a realization of the true self. Self-realization in this system means to become aware of the divine within oneself (*Brahman*). Yoga is considered to be an instrument that brings a person to the point of recognizing the supposedly divine core of one's being.

Rama Jyoti Vernon, founder of Unity in Yoga International and the California Yoga Teachers' Association in the U.S., sees the postures of yoga as a way to become one with the "eternal cosmic vibration." Through yoga, one withdraws to the mountaintop to seek his own salvation and enlightenment, she says.[20]

Common explanations by gurus and yoga instructors would describe yoga as a way to enter the soul through an inward journey. They describe yoga as a way to clear distractions and obstacles in a person's consciousness -- in other words to empty oneself, and therefore come to a point of abiding in one's supposedly true divine nature. They say that yoga connects a person with the universe, teaches one about self, and gives one energy to know eternity. Tony Quinn, founder of numerous yoga conference centers in Ireland, states the goal of yoga as self-expression and self-realization, which he explains as mystically experiencing one's true identity and finding it to be divine (*Brahman*).[21] Essentially this view is not different and boils down to the assumption that mankind has within himself everything he needs to be united with god. He just needs to realize his supposedly divine nature.

Yoga instructor Diane Barnes describes the aim of yoga as yoking the consciousness of love with the divine. She sees her goal as a yoga instructor to help people find the place within themselves where they can connect with the higher consciousness of the divine. Barnes further says, "The practice of yoga enables people to come to a point of faith as they have a direct experience of operating on faith."[22]

The biblical perspective of union with God is very different. According to the Bible, the believer's relationship with God is not instigated through self-realization, but rather through faith in Jesus' sacrificial death and resurrection from the dead, which made the way so human beings could draw close to God and have a personal relationship with Him, "for God so loved the world that he gave his one and only Son, that whoever believes in him shall not perish but have eternal life" (John 3:16). This relationship is described as a relationship of trust and intimacy, similar to that of a close friendship. The system of yoga portrays god as an impersonal force that exists in all of creation and basically means that everything is divine. This concept of god, as stated before, comes directly from Hinduism and is called *Brahman,* which is understood to be the ultimate reality, the principle that underlies everything.

The Bible, however, says that there are no other gods besides the one true God, who created heaven and earth and everything in it, and it is for this very reason that the pantheistic worldview that everything is divine, which is held by most yoga propagators, cannot be justified on biblical grounds. In the Bible God portrays Himself as the creator of the universe who is distinct and separate, and yet very involved with His creation (Gen. 1:26). He is a personal God who wants to relate with human beings, not just a force or an underlying principle of reality. Therefore the concept of the divine as it is often found within yoga is very unlike the God of the Bible.

Yoga appears to be another example of what happened in the Garden of Eden, when man was seduced by Satan's suggestion that he could be like God, saying, "For God knows that when you eat of it your eyes will be opened, and you will be like God, knowing good and evil" (Gen. 3:5). The system of yoga brings this concept to a climax by suggesting that man's only problem is his failure to recognize his godhood within self. Christian authors Dave Hunt and T.A. McMahon make this point clear, saying, "Satan reinforces his promise of godhood with the lie that we have all we need within us. If we only know how to get in touch with our true self, then we can tap into this power."[23] In addition, Hunt and McMahon point out:

> *The goal of yoga is "self-realization" to look deeply within what ought to be the temple of the one true God and there to discover the alleged "true Self" or "higher Self" and declare self to be God. This is the religion of Antichrist; and for the first time in history it is being widely practiced throughout the Western world as Transcendental Meditation and other forms of yoga.[24]*

Taking into consideration all these different aspects, the conviction emerges that the focus in yoga is clearly on what man can do to find god. It assumes that a person can return to god through his own efforts. Within this system lies the inherent danger of suggesting what is not true, that human beings have the power to make peace with god by applying certain techniques and that by trying hard to remove distractions they can focus on their inner self and find it to be divine. Yoga can lead a person to a misconceived idea of what god is like, which blinds him towards the fact that God is a personal God who desires a personal relationship with human beings.

This personal relationship with God is the real, and most important, need of any human being.

Armin Weidle

Chapter Six

Yoga and Original Sin

The concept of original sin within yoga is very closely interwoven with the Hindu view, which proposes that man is basically good because he supposedly has divine potential within himself, and that original sin does not exist. In Hinduism sin is also often seen as merely external, more like wrong deeds, and not as something inherent in human nature. Through ritual cleansing or meditation a person can make up for their errors and can become clean. Though differing views of sin are held in yoga circles, they all have one thing in common: sin is not man's ultimate problem, but a lack of self-realization is. Even yoga proponents who do talk about the existence of sin promote a works approach as a remedy, acknowledging man as a sinner, but saying that man can improve himself and his standing before god through good works. Often, sinful behavior is associated with the belief that the mind of a person has not been emptied and therefore unified with body and soul yet, and that the person still needs to deal with these "distractions of the mind." Consider what Yogi Maharishi Mahesh said concerning this matter: "[Meditation] brings us more ability for achieving something through right means, and very easily a sinner comes out of the field of sin and becomes a virtuous man."[25] Ravi Ravindra also stresses the works-mentality of yoga: "Agitation in any part of the entire organism causes fluctuations in attention and muddies the seeing. This is the reason why in yoga there is so much emphasis on the preparation of the body for coming to true knowledge."[26]

Other yoga proponents like Sri Swami Chidananda, former president of the Divine Life Society in Rishikesh, India, and author of numerous books on Hindu philosophy and yoga, deny the existence of sin altogether. He stated,

It differs [yoga vs. Christianity] in its refusing to accept the doctrine of "original sin." It does not call man a sinner. It may call man a fool but it doesn't call him a sinner. Man is god playing the fool, or, man is god who has lost his way home, wandered away, stumbling and running about in circles. It [yoga] clears up the path, puts light and puts man on the path again and says, "go ahead now, go straight to your home." So it doesn't want you to consider yourself a sinner.[27]

Chidananda continues by explaining yoga's understanding of heaven and hell. "Yoga rejects hell, and yoga rejects heaven also...yoga concerns itself with god, not heaven or hell."[28]

Because yoga denies sin or takes a works approach to resolve it, it also denies the fact that a great price needed to be paid to make human beings right with God again. The Bible is very clear in stating that the nature of human beings is sinful and that there is no one without sin, "for all have sinned and fall short of the glory of God" (Rom. 3:23). In Ps. 51:5 it says, "Behold, I was brought forth in iniquity, And in sin my mother conceived me" (NKJV). Therefore, the view of sin within yoga is in contradiction to that of the Bible. It becomes clear that even in this aspect, yoga can be an instrument to lead man away from the revealed truth of the God of the Bible.

Chapter Seven

Yoga and the Occult

Could there be any links of yoga with the occult? Is yoga occultic in itself, or can involvement in yoga be an inroad to occult practices? The *Webster's New World College Dictionary* defines "occult" as something involving the mystical or esoteric. The word "occult" comes from the Latin word *occultus* which means to cover up, to hide or address things that are hidden or done in secret.[29] Terms associated with the occult are black art, black magic, diabolism, occultism, sorcery and witchcraft. Occultism focuses on gaining psychic knowledge and power and attempts to control the forces of nature (also called life energy).

Psychic energy is also an element that can be found in yoga. Johanna Michaelsen comments on psychic energy in Hatha Yoga:

What the practice of Hatha Yoga is designed to do is suppress the flow of psychic energies through these channels ["supposed energy channels on either side of the spinal column"], thereby forcing the "serpent power" or the kundalini force to rise through the central psychic channel in the spine (the sushumna) and up through the chakras, the supposed psychic centers of human personality and power.[30]

In their research about yoga, Dr. Ankerberg and Dr. Weldon confirm that psychic power is an element of yoga. They found that "certain experiences under yoga (especially Kundalini Yoga) are similar to those found in shaman initiation and ritualistic magic, including experiences of spirit possession and insanity. Virtually all standard yoga texts acknowledge that yoga practice develops psychic powers and other occult abilities."[31] The fact that *kundalini* is described as psychic energy that is located at the base of the spine and can be aroused through Kundalini Yoga or other forms of yoga, could also be a hint to its connection with the occult. In addition, there are commonalities between the effects of occult practices on a person, and those of *kundalini*.

One expert on this topic is Gopi Krishna, a respected authority on *kundalini*, who during his lifetime promoted the scientific investigation of it and believed that human beings could reach higher consciousness through *kundalini*. Gopi Krishna knew the effects of *kundalini* very well and in his book, *Living with Kundalini*, he illustrates some of them:

Unless the mind has been disciplined from an early age, a stimulated kundalini brings with it an irrepressible desire for the occult and the bizarre. It is incredible to what extent the victims of this desire can be duped by pseudo-Godmen, charlatans and imposters. It appears as if the mind has lost all its critical power of observing and judging the behavior of an individual whom people credit with psychic powers. They act in the most abnormal and revolting ways, which the duped audiences ascribe to mystical consciousness, transcending normal actions.[32]

Krishna further states the arousal of *kundalini* can cause a "desire for strange drug experiences, for erratic psychic phenomena, for fantastic messages received from mediums and sensitives, [and] for the strange actions of gurus and occult teachers."[33]

According to Kundalini Yoga practitioners, *kundalini* can be utilized and directed to the brain, where it is supposed to cause intense feelings of divine bliss and mental ease. The problem is that a lot of those practitioners do not warn their clients about the dangerous side of Kundalini Yoga. Guru Swami Narayanananda described some of the dangers as:

[The arousal of *kundalini* involves] *hot currents that reach the brain center, heat the brain, make the mind fickle, bring insomnia, brain disorder, insanity and incurable diseases. For the hot currents keep the mind wide awake and if a person does not know how to check the currents and to bring down the partly risen kundalini shakti [serpent power or female energy] to safe centers, one suffers terribly and it may ruin the whole life of a person or lead one to insanity. This is why we see so many become insane, many get brain defects, and many others get some incurable diseases.*[34]

41

Rabindranath Maharaj, a former guru and devoted Hindu, now a follower of Christ, says this about *kundalini*:

> *When aroused without proper control, it* [the *kundalini*] *rages like a vicious serpent inside a person with a force that is impossible to resist. It is said that without proper control, the kundalini will produce supernatural psychic powers having their source in demonic beings and will lead ultimately to moral, spiritual, and physical destruction. Nevertheless it is this kundalini power that meditation and yoga are designed to arouse . . . .*[35]

This shows that the effects of Kundalini Yoga and the involved arousal of the *kundalini* energy are dangerous. The commonalities of the effects of *kundalini* and those of occult practices are striking. Not only can *kundalini* overtake a person and do permanent damage to him, but there is also the possibility that the person will lose any sound judgment and become a slave to this force. These are all patterns that would be characteristic of many occult practices as well.

Destructive effects of *kundalini* are also confirmed by people who either were involved in Kundalini Yoga themselves or had close contact with people who were. A former yoga practitioner Mineda J. McCleave describes her experience with Kundalini Yoga:

> *I plunged into meditative prayer . . . I began to have*

problems relating to the world around me. I had shifts in consciousness during my non-meditative hours . . . I was again bothered with alternating periods of euphoria, anxiety, depression, and, sometimes, despair. I was surprised to find that my peaceful prayer life was often counterbalanced with thoughts of suicide. I could not understand these strange moods . . . . This activity, added to long periods of prayer, was causing changes, painful ones, in my mind and body. The physical, mental, and emotional problems that surfaced were so dramatic that I had to quit working. I withdrew from society and had to rely upon my family to care for and support me . . . I had begun a long 'dark night of the soul', and it lasted for ten years. Finally, in 1975 when I was thirty-seven years old, I was hospitalized three times in the psychiatric ward of the local hospital . . . I could no longer cope with my agitated mind. I was besieged with migraine headaches and no longer had any control over my life.[36]

She goes on to explain, "My mind was hyperactive . . . physically, I went through a variety of symptoms . . . emotionally, I went up and down the keyboard of euphoria, joy, bewilderment, anxiety, depression, and the familiar despair. I was at times deluded and often disoriented. On one occasion, I actually believed I had died."[37] What started out with some seemingly harmless yoga classes clearly led McCleave into a destructive cycle, which severely harmed her body, her emotions, and had negative effects upon her family as well. In addition to practitioners, some yoga instructors also warn about destructive effects of Kundalini Yoga. Marja Savola, founder of the Kundalini Information and Network website, is one of them. She also warns:

> *Another of my clients had a divine experience, and in the session after that she began to levitate (rise) from the bed with the upper part of the body. At the same time she rattled and gasped for breath as if she was dying. (I later found out in my Indian books, that she already had started a kundalini arousal in her third session - this was her tenth - and she actually could have died!) Other side effects had been enormous heat and she prespired [sic] a lot. Sometimes she even had fever the next day following a session.*[38]

These and more examples that could be mentioned should be a warning of the possible destructive effects of Kundalini Yoga. The question if yoga is occult still remains. Yoga can certainly be an inroad for a person to eventually get involved in other occult practices, but is yoga occult in itself? To answer this question we must go back to the *Webster's* definition of the word "occult." Yoga definitely entails the mystical, and the esoteric, which would qualify yoga as "occult." However, we also need to look at spiritual realities that are involved. The only true path to seek the supernatural as revealed in the Bible is by approaching God directly through Jesus Christ. To seek supernatural or spiritual knowledge apart from this path is very dangerous, because Satan creates a counterfeit spirituality or even supernatural manifestations to satisfy our longing to get in touch with the supernatural. By doing that he creates a trap to bring people into bondage to his kingdom of darkness.

Even though it often cannot be seen, there is a spiritual reality in this world. According to the Bible there are two kinds of spirits in the spiritual realm, the Spirit of God (Holy Spirit) and the spirit of the antichrist. Everything that is not in line with God's character and does not acknowledge Jesus as Christ is the spirit of the antichrist, "and every spirit that does not confess that Jesus Christ has come in the flesh is not of God. And this is the spirit of the Antichrist, which you have heard was coming, and is now already in the world" (1 John 4:3 NKJV). The nature of the Spirit of God is life, but the nature of the spirit of the antichrist is death.

The Spirit of God aims to lead human beings to a humble submission to God that leads to life, while the spirit of the antichrist operates to cause rebellion against God, which ultimately leads to death (Rom. 6:16). Whenever something is occult, it is the spirit of the antichrist at work, whose aim is to bring about death in a person's life.

Yoga is derived from Hinduism, and neither the system of yoga nor Hinduism acknowledges Jesus as the only way to God. Yoga is designed to draw people who practice it to seek the supernatural in ways other than coming to God directly through Jesus Christ. Various techniques are used, depending on the type of yoga, to get in touch with the inner self

45

with the hope of finding God. This is also true for Hatha Yoga which may not seem to aim at getting in touch with the supernatural at first, as discussed earlier, but is still designed to do exactly that. That is why there is still a danger that even people who are not intentionally seeking the supernatural by doing yoga at first, may over time gradually be affected by its spiritual nature.

In closing this chapter, I want to stress that inherent in yoga are clear spiritual implications that are derived from Hinduism, which are in opposition to the truth of the Bible. It is obvious that the spirit of the antichrist is at work within yoga and altogether the facts from above show clearly that yoga is occult at its core.

PART THREE

Christian Applications

Armin Weidle

Chapter Eight

Can Yoga Be Christian?

More and more we hear the term "Christian Yoga" and the number of its advocates are growing. What do they mean by Christian Yoga?

Jean-Marie Dechanet, a French monk, believes in Christian Yoga and says that yoga can be disconnected from the Hindu objective of self-realization. Dechanet suggests replacing "self" with a different object of meditation, such as God, and talks about the use of a body language of prayer as one's prayers to God. Dechanet sees those prayers symbolically supported through the use of yoga postures. He says, "The bruising of the joints can be made to serve as a springboard for the Spirit, particularly for someone striving to live a Christian life."[39] Christian Yoga author Louis Hughes agrees with Dechanet, but adds, "Nevertheless I would also maintain that some (but by no means all) yogic techniques can be beneficially utilized to dispose a person to a fuller experience of Christian prayer and living."[40] Christian Yoga proponent and author

Nancy Roth states at the beginning of her book, *An Invitation to Christian Yoga*:

> *This book presents one particular way of opening ourselves to the wholeness and holiness that is the gift of God in Christ, as we seek to relearn the unity of "body-spirit". It is the way based on Hatha Yoga, which was developed in the ancient Hindu tradition. Because we practice it within the Christian context, we call it "Christian Yoga."*[41]

Roth even incorporates Hindu prayer terminology, saying that "favorite *mantras* include 'Jesus Christ', 'My Lord and my God', 'Holy Spirit', 'Be still and know that I am God', or merely the word 'God.'"[42] According to Roth, Hatha Yoga can be utilized and incorporated into a Christian context. She believes that yoga can add to the experience of a Christian and sees no conflict with the combination of Christianity and yoga.

Yoga instructor Susan Bordenkircher from Alabama also teaches Christian Yoga. She produced a Christian Yoga video series called *Outstretched in Worship*. Bordenkircher believes that through Christian Yoga the two goals of becoming physically healthy and spiritually healthy can be combined.[43]

If you are a Christian, you may have to make a decision at some point if Christian Yoga is something that you could do for exercise or meditation. In other words, you might ask if yoga can be filled with Christian meaning and if it's okay for you to practice it. Considering some foundational facts might help you in making that decision. We discussed earlier that the yoga postures (*asanas*) are designed to convey Hindu meaning. That means they were created to give reference to a Hindu god who is completely different from the God of the Bible. If the *asanas* are used in a Christian context they still convey their original Hindu meaning, even when combined with words or concepts from the Bible.

God clearly told His people that they shouldn't make covenants with the pagan nations around them, nor with their gods (Exod. 23:32). If you are practicing Christian Yoga, you are making a covenant with Hindu gods, knowingly or unknowingly. Just because Christian meaning is added to yoga doesn't mean that the Hindu meaning is removed or will not have any influence upon the person who practices it. Hindu philosophy is such an integral part of yoga that it cannot be completely separated from it, not even in Christian Yoga. Giving reference to Hindu gods means bowing to other gods instead of the true God who created everything. He is the only one worthy of worship (Deut. 29:17-18).

Before the people of Israel entered the land that God had promised them, He told them the following, "You shall not bow down to their gods, nor serve them, nor do according to their works; but you shall utterly overthrow them and completely break down their sacred pillars" (Exod. 23:24 NKJV). According to God's word a Christian should revere no other gods besides the one true God (Exod. 20:3-5). He is the only one worthy of worship. To give reference to Hindu gods, even when one might not be doing it consciously, is not God's will for any Christian. God wants us to worship Him in spirit and truth (John 4:24). His word is truth (John 17:17). Therefore, it is very clear that mixing elements of Hinduism into one's worship is not pleasing to God. Thus, yoga cannot be Christian and the term "Christian Yoga" is a paradox in itself.

Chapter Nine

Alternatives to Yoga

As mentioned earlier, yoga does have various physical benefits, yet because of its spiritual dangers that outweigh those benefits, I would like to offer alternatives to yoga and yoga postures.

Fitness expert Laurette Willis has developed a great alternative to yoga called PraiseMoves®. The stretching postures of PraiseMoves® are linked to Scriptures from the Bible which are meditated upon, thus renewing the mind and refreshing the spirit while gently exercising the body. Laurette designed postures such as the "Eagle" (Isa. 40:31), the "Rainbow" (Gen. 9:16) and the "Angel" (Ps. 91:11), to name a few. These gentle stretches provide all the physical benefits of yoga without opening a person up to the spiritual realm of Hinduism or New Age. PraiseMoves® can help a person to improve flexibility, to assist weight loss, to incorporate full-body stretching, to alleviate stress, to heal injuries, to improve coordination and agility, and to keep the tissues healthier.

A PraiseMoves® class consists of five sections, which are called PraiseMoves® "Walkin' Wisdom

Warm-ups", PraiseMoves® Postures, PraiseMoves® Scripture Sequences, PraiseMoves® Alphabetics, and WWJD Meditation Relaxation.[44]

1. **PraiseMoves® "Walkin' Wisdom Warm-ups"** are a warm-up of the muscles through walking in place to lively gospel music while proclaiming Scripture out loud. They are an optional preparation for the PraiseMoves® workout.

2. **PraiseMoves® Postures** are a series of gentle postures to increase flexibility and muscle strength, which are integrated with Scripture.

3. **PraiseMoves® Scripture Sequences** are built into doing the postures after 10-15 minutes. For example Scriptures like "The Lord's prayer" or Psalm 23 are recited. The postures and Scripture correspond with each other, while the postures underline the meaning of Scripture.

4. **PraiseMoves® Alphabetics** are postures which correspond to the 22 letters of the Hebrew Alphabet, Aleph through Tav. For each class the instructor chooses a letter and postures that mirror that letter. While the participants are doing the postures, they listen to the corresponding portion of Psalm 119. This Psalm is an acrostic poem with 22 stanzas, one

for each letter of the Hebrew alphabet.

5. **WWJD Meditation/Relaxation** are a section where participants rest on the floor for a few minutes and think about a proverb, portion of Scripture, or a Psalm with the goal to focus on what Jesus wants them to do.

For more information about Praise Moves® go to www.PraiseMoves.com.

Other resources for stretches that don't have anything to do with yoga can be found at: http://www.womenswheartfoundation.org/content/Exercise/stretching_exercise.asp. Or you can purchase "The Stretch Deck," an illustrated card set of fifty stretches by Olivia Miller and Nicole Kaufman. It can be purchased over the Internet from many major booksellers.

Another alternative to yoga is something I call Meditative Stretching. It can help a person to achieve similar physical benefits without doing the yoga postures that convey Hindu meaning, and to get a well-rounded workout of body, soul, and mind.

The purpose of Meditative Stretching is to help you stretch your body and draw you closer to God. In Meditative Stretching the focus is outward on God, rather than inward on self. The goal in Meditative Stretching is not to empty one's mind like in yoga, but to fill the mind with life-changing truth, as well as to get a balanced and gentle workout of the whole body. The meditation part of Meditative Stretching is designed to fill one's mind with truth, which could be done by focusing on an attribute of God like His holiness, love, compassion, or righteousness, or one of His names, combined with a corresponding verse from the Bible. You can also focus on a truth that God has brought to your attention concerning your life and that He wants you to experience. For example, words like love, joy, peace, patience, kindness, goodness, faithfulness, gentleness, and self-control could be used as keywords along with a Bible verse that supports the word. As you meditate, keep in mind that meditation means contemplating who God is.

In order to combine your meditation with stretching it is best to use gentle stretching exercises. The key is to stretch slowly and gently and not to overstretch. I recommend that you stretch after your meditation so you can continue thinking about what became important to you or what God told you during your meditation.

Gentle and soft instrumental music or nature sounds may help you to relax and be more at ease while doing Meditative Stretching. Meditative Stretching will help you to get a healthy and balanced workout, and it will combine those benefits with drawing you closer to the true God of the universe and help you get to know Him better. Only when all of those aspects are combined, can maximum stress reduction, physical wellness and spiritual health be achieved.

In both of the above-mentioned alternatives to yoga, meditation and drawing close to God are the central elements. Whether you have had a personal relationship with God for a short time or a long time, or you are seeking to know Him for the first time, do you really know how to meditate and walk with God more closely? Many times yoga becomes attractive, especially to Christians, because they have never experienced deep and fulfilling meditation. To experience fulfilling meditation is not easy, but with some effort and God's help you can learn to meditate and enjoy closeness with God without entering into the realm of Hinduism or New Age. There are plenty of techniques for good meditation. The essence of it is rather basic: to learn to listen to God and to hear His still, soft voice.

True meditation is not about emptying one's mind, but about focusing it on God, and to fill it with truth in regard to what God is saying concerning Himself and every aspect of life. One tool to help do that is the Psalms. They are great windows into the inner lives of people who were intimate with God, who knew how to draw close to Him and drink deeply from His fountain of life-giving water. I especially recommend Psalms 42 and 131, but there are many other Psalms that are also excellent for meditation. I also recommend a good book on meditation called *Celebration of Discipline*, by Richard Foster, published by Harper & Row. It includes instruction and examples from the Bible on meditation.

Through these practical examples a believer can learn how to have a more intimate relationship with God. This will certainly be an experience that is far more fulfilling than in yoga. Another great resource to learn how to enter into the presence of God and know Him more deeply is a book called *Secrets of the Secret Place*, written by Bob Sorge and published by Oasis House. In this book you find fifty-two short chapters that can be an excellent help with meditation.

When you are seeking to meditate and know God more deeply, remember that God promises us that if we draw close to Him, He will draw close to us (Jas. 4:8). God is looking for worshipers who will worship Him in spirit and truth (John 4:23, 24). Even when it is a struggle to enjoy undistracted closeness with God, know that God is by your side. It pleases Him when His children are seeking fellowship with Him. When you ask God for help in this struggle, He won't hide from you, but will graciously lead you to greater depths of intimacy with Him.

Chapter Ten

Talking About Yoga With Loved Ones

Since yoga is very popular and people who practice it do so for specific benefits, it may not be easy to point out its negative aspects to friends and family. Here are a few suggestions to keep in mind when you discuss yoga.

First of all, it is important that you ask questions about why the person practices yoga. Try to understand them and their motives and what they like about yoga. Recognize that they are benefiting from yoga in some way.

After the person has had sufficient time to talk about yoga, why it is important to them, and how they benefit from it, ask them if you could share some information about the roots of yoga. Depending on their answers and their reasons why they practice yoga, you can share some of the information about the roots of yoga, using questions to talk about different aspects.

For example, you could ask if your loved one has thought about what the roots of yoga are. What do they think is the meaning and the purpose of the yoga postures? You can also ask them about their yoga class and whether Hinduism is discussed in class. If Hindu thought is not discussed in class, and their purpose for practicing yoga is mainly exercise, stress relief, or health benefits, you could ask them whether they realize that they may be impacted by Hinduism through their yoga practice. If this surprises them you should explain how even the practice of yoga only with the purpose of exercise, stress relief, or for its health benefits, could still be an inroad for Hinduism to influence their life.

Never try to push anything on your loved ones. After you ask a couple of questions and they seem open and interested in talking, you can go on with sharing more. If the person doesn't want to hear any of the information that you have to share about yoga, you should never force it on them.

Anytime you force something it might actually accomplish the opposite of what you intended, and your loved one might engage in yoga more than before. If your loved one is interested in talking about this topic, you can also briefly tell them about this book and offer to share it with them. In case your loved one is looking for alternatives to yoga, tell them that there are some good options and share some of the alternatives with them.

Chapter Eleven

Conclusion

The goal of this book was to investigate and show the truth about the roots and fruits of yoga as it is most practiced in the Western world (specifically Hatha Yoga and Kundalini Yoga). We looked at various facets in order to shed more light on the fruits of yoga. By looking at these different facets, it became clear that yoga is not innocent, as some would argue who see it only as an exercise. Even Hatha Yoga, which is a subordination of Raja Yoga, cannot be considered just physical exercise, because it is clearly part of the whole system of yoga and also aims to draw people into the spiritual realm. This can be a subtle and longer process but nevertheless the fact remains that Hatha Yoga still has Hinduism at its core and cannot be disconnected from it.

We also discovered how yoga affects the human mind. This is an important aspect, as the mind is the main target of Satan for attacking people and keeping them from living in a close relationship with God. By looking at the effects of yoga on the mind, the conviction emerged that yoga is designed to instill Hindu thinking patterns that can lead people into bondage to Satan.

It also became clear that the yoga of the West stands for a New Age concept of god, where god is viewed as an impersonal force that exists within the whole of creation. That is why in this system of thought, people are encouraged to come to a realization that they are divine, and to remove distractions through yoga to experience the divine within themselves.

With regard to original sin, the research showed that sin is either denied within the system of yoga or it is not viewed as mankind's main problem. It is rather stated that human beings just need to come to a realization of their inner self (*atman*) and they will discover their true self of supposedly being divine.

We also discussed some of the destructive effects that yoga can have and whether yoga is an occult practice in itself or if it can lead a person to occult practices. Through case studies that showed occult manifestations in people's lives caused by involvement in yoga, a word definition of the occult, and looking at spiritual realities according to the Bible, it became obvious that yoga is at its core an occult practice. The spirit of death is clearly at the core of the yoga system and therefore it is a tricky scheme of Satan to draw people into bondage to his destructive purposes.

In addition, it became clear that in Christian Yoga, one might try to add Christian meaning to yoga with the purpose of retaining its physical benefits and trying to remove its mental and spiritual aspects. It is key, though, that even in Christian Yoga, yoga still cannot be disconnected from what it was originally designed for -- to pay tribute to Hindu gods.

Lastly, I suggested two alternatives to yoga that do not have anything to do with yoga but offer similar physical benefits and can lift a person spiritually by conveying spiritual truth. They are called PraiseMoves® and Meditative Stretching.

It is possible for a person to depend on yoga rather than the true and living God and therefore exalt yoga to a position in their lives that in reality only their creator God can have. When yoga takes the place of God in a person's life it becomes an idol as if they are "bowing to yoga", instead of giving reference and honor to the only one who is worthy of that, the true and living God.

Chapter Twelve

Life With God

As a writer and follower of Jesus who has been concerned about the dangers of yoga for a number of years, it is my prayer that you would be informed and learn to understand the inherent dangers of practicing yoga. My hope is for you to realize that seemingly harmless yoga classes can affect you in very negative ways. I pray that you would see that yoga is designed to lead you down a destructive path and to keep you from a relationship with the true and living God, who wants to give you lasting peace and joy in your life as a free gift through faith in Jesus Christ because of His great love for you.

If you are inspired by this book and wonder how you can find true life and real fellowship with God, these last paragraphs are for you! The Bible says in Romans 3:23 (NLT), "For all have sinned; all fall short of God's glorious standard." This is the problem of every human being. God is perfectly holy and we cannot stand before God, because we are not perfect and naturally do not live up to His standard.

We ourselves want to be at the center of our world and focus on self rather than on God. The Bible also makes it clear in Romans 6:23 (NKJV), "For the wages of sin is death, but the gift of God is eternal life in Christ Jesus our Lord." This means that the outcome of this old path is separation from God in this life on earth and ultimately separation from Him in eternity, which means eternal death. If we continue in this path, we miss out on the life that we were created for, to have fellowship with God in this life and to be in His presence for eternity. Eternal death and the absence of God's presence for eternity are much worse than we can imagine.

In God's Word, in the parable of the rich man and Lazarus, this outcome is described as a place of torment and never-ending fire: "In hell, where he [the rich man] was in torment, he looked up and saw Abraham far away, with Lazarus by his side. So he called to him, 'Father Abraham, have pity on me and send Lazarus to dip the tip of his finger in water and cool my tongue, because I am in agony in this fire" (Luke 16:23-24).

There is hope, though, as mentioned in Romans 10:9 (NLT), "For if you confess with your mouth that Jesus is Lord and believe in your heart that God raised him from the dead, you will be saved." God promises eternal life to everyone who turns from his old way of life, turns to Him in faith, and believes in his heart that Jesus died for his sin. John 3:16 (NKJV) says, "For God so loved the world that He gave His only begotten Son [Jesus Christ], that whoever believes in Him should not perish but have everlasting life."

If you believe that, and sincerely want to

commit your life to Jesus, to do His will instead of your own will from now on, you can pray a prayer similar to this one:

"Dear Jesus, I know that I fall short of your glorious standard, but I want to change. I know that in my own strength I cannot change, but I believe in my heart that you died for my sin on the cross and that you are alive now. I want to commit my life to you and follow you for the rest of my life. Amen."

If you did commit your life to Jesus, I encourage you to find a good Bible believing and Spirit filled church, where you can have fellowship with other Christians and grow in your faith. If you are unsure how to find a good church, please contact me at bowing2yoga@gmail.com and I will try to help you find one in your area.

Final Thoughts

The fact that you read this book shows me that you are interested in yoga in one way or another. Maybe you came across yoga through a friend or family member who is involved in it, or you heard about it in the media. Perhaps you read this book to find out what yoga is really all about and to get answers to some of your questions, or you looked into it because you were planning to get involved, but were not sure if you could do so with peace of mind. In any case, I hope that you were able to get some answers to your questions and that you have a clearer picture now of what yoga is all about and what its roots and fruits are.

My intention in writing this book was to provide a truthful foundation about yoga, as I have seen much written on yoga, but little that really presented the truth about its roots and fruits. If you have read this book to help you with a decision about yoga, such as whether to get involved in it yourself or to advise someone else who is contemplating that, you will face a decision of what to do with the information in this book. My purpose was to give you the facts about yoga and show you what it is all about. I leave it up to you what to do with this information but do want to encourage you to give it enough thought and pray about it before you do make a decision. I myself have decided that I will not engage in any form of yoga and would not advise anyone to do so.

There are still a lot of questions that remain concerning the effects of modern yoga, and there is tremendous need for further research and publication of written material in this area. The brain activity during the practice of yoga especially needs to be looked at more thoroughly from a medical standpoint, and there is a need for Christian professionals to work on this, since they are the only ones who can base their findings on a proper spiritual foundation. Also, the process of the development of yoga into its modern forms is an area where further research and writing is needed.

For comments or questions on this book, feel free to contact me at: bowing2yoga@gmail.com.

Appendix

How To Know God And Receive Eternal Life
Glossary Of Terms
Notes
Resources
About the Author

Armin Weidle

How to know God and receive eternal life

Jesus came to this world, died on the cross and rose from the dead so that human beings could know God and have a personal relationship with Him. Jesus says this about himself:

> **John 14:6 (NLT) I am the way, the truth, and the life. No one can come to the Father except through me.**

The condition of every person who is born is described like this:

> **Romans 3:23 (NLT) For all have sinned; all fall short of God's glorious standard.**

God is perfectly holy without any blemish, and He cannot tolerate sin. Because the first human beings Adam and Eve made a decision against God, every human being is born with a sinful nature that separates them from God. By our own efforts we all miss the mark of God's perfect holiness.

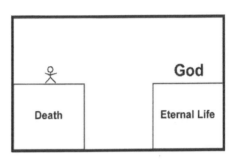

This would be really bad news, but fortunately there is good news as well:

Romans 6:23 (NKJV) For the wages of sin is death, but the gift of God is eternal life in Christ Jesus our Lord.

John 3:16 (NKJV) For God so loved the world that He gave His only begotten Son, that whoever believes in Him should not perish but have everlasting life.

God loves us so much and wants to have a relationship with us, so he provided a way by giving His Son Jesus as an offering for our sin. Jesus died in our place and made a way for us to be accepted by God. Because Jesus was the only one on earth who lived a sinless life, he was the only one who could be a substitute.

Even though a follower of Jesus is still not

perfect and never will be in this life, through Jesus he can now draw close to God and have a personal relationship with Him.

1 Peter 3:18 (NLT) Christ also suffered when He died for our sins once for all time. He never sinned, but he died for sinners that he might bring us safely home to God. He suffered physical death, but he was raised to life in the Spirit.

Because of our sinful nature and God's perfect holiness, we cannot draw close to Him without Jesus. Without Jesus we couldn't enjoy the presence of God in this life nor in eternity, but would only be left to eternal suffering in the lake of fire after this life and be forever separated from God.

When someone believes in Jesus, though, and allows him to be Lord over his life, Jesus becomes the bridge that will enable that person to have fellowship with God in this life and to spend eternity in the presence of God in perfect fellowship with Him.

John 11:25-26 (NKJV) [Jesus says,] "I am the resurrection and the life. He who believes in Me, though he may die, he shall live."

How To Receive The Son And The Free Gift Of Eternal Life

◆ NOT BY HUMAN EFFORT

No human effort, be it by doing good things, living a moral life, or through a religious works approach, can help you to have the Son and the free gift of eternal life. According to God's perspective, we are all completely helpless in that respect. It was only through God's mercy that He made a way for us to know Him.

> **Ephesians 2:8-9 (NLT) God saved you by his special favor when you believed. And you can't take credit for this; it is a gift from God. Salvation is not a reward for the good things we have done, so none of us can boast about it.**
>
> **Romans 5:6 (NLT) When we were utterly helpless, Christ came at just the right time and died for us sinners.**
>
> **Romans 5:8 (NLT) But God showed His great love for us by sending Christ to die for us while we were still sinners.**

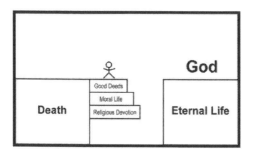

◆ ONLY BY FAITH IN JESUS

We cannot earn a right standing with God. It is God's gift to us. The question is whether we accept it. How can we accept this gift of God?

Romans 10:9 (NLT) For if you confess with your mouth that Jesus is Lord and believe in your heart that God raised him from the dead, you will be saved.

So we see that faith is the key aspect. When we believe with all our heart that Jesus died on the cross for our sin and was raised three days later from the grave, then we can be sure that we will be with Him in eternity. This kind of faith is not merely intellectual, but comes from deep within the heart. It is the beginning of a growing relationship with God so that we really can know Him in an intimate way.

John 17:3 (NKJV) "And this is eternal life, that they may know You, the only true God, and Jesus Christ whom You have sent."

1 John 5:11-12 (NLT) And this is what God has testified: He has given us eternal life, and this life is in his Son. So whoever has God's Son has life; whoever does not have his Son does not have life.

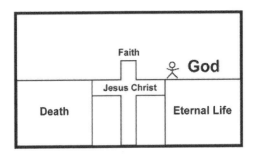

♦ **YOUR DECISION**

If you are ready to make a decision to live in a personal relationship with God and allow Jesus to be Lord over your life, you can do so by simply telling Him. This decision should be made with all your heart. Lip service alone won't do it.

Before you make this most important decision of your life, you should also know what it involves. In Luke 14:26-33 Jesus tells a story about what is involved when someone wants to follow Him. This story might sound harsh at first and you might ask if Jesus really meant that we should hate our father and mother and children and brothers and sisters and our own life and that we should give up all of our possessions in order to follow Him.

Luke 14:26-33 (NKJV) If anyone comes to Me and does not hate his father and mother, wife and children, brothers and sisters, yes, and his own life also, he cannot be My disciple. 27 And whoever does not bear his cross and come after Me cannot be my disciple. 28 For which of you, intending to build a tower, does not sit down first, and count the cost, whether he has enough to finish it- 29 lest, after he has laid the foundation, and is not able to finish, all who see it begin to mock him, 30 saying, 'This man began to build, and was not able to finish'?. 31 Or what king, going to make war against another king, does not sit down first and consider whether he is able with ten thousand to meet him who comes against him with twenty thousand? 32 Or else, while the other is still a great way off, he sends a delegation and asks conditions of peace. 33 So likewise, whoever of you does not forsake all that he has cannot be My disciple.

In those verses Jesus illustrates a principle of what it means to follow Him and allow Him to direct our life. It means that we put Jesus first in our life, that we surrender completely to His will, and allow nothing else to interfere with that.

This might sound really harsh to you now, but remember that Jesus loves you so much that He died for you. God wants our best, even when at times we might not see that at first. God promises us:

> *For I know the thoughts that I think toward you, says the Lord, thoughts of peace and not of evil, to give you a future and a hope. Jeremiah 29:11 (NKJV)*

Glossary Of Terms

Asanas

The postures of yoga. They have different shapes and convey specific Hindu meanings.

Ashtanga Yoga

A form of Hatha Yoga also known as Power Yoga. Students jump from one posture to another to build strength, stamina, and flexibility, while practicing breath control at the same time.

Atman

Considered an underlying metaphysical self. Some scholars interpret it as as the "main essence" of man, or his highest self.

Bhagavad-Gita, or "The Song of the Lord"

A Hindu scripture which is a part of India's national epic poem, the *Mahabarata*. As a core sacred text of Hinduism and philosophy, the Bhagavad Gita, often referred to as the Gita, is a summation of the Vedic, Yogic, Vedantic, and Tantric philosophies.

Bhakti Yoga

One of the four major yogic paths of

Hinduism. It focuses on devotion and emphasizes surrender to the supreme cosmic spirit through prayer, worship and ritual, channeling, and transmuting emotions into unconditional love or devotion.

Bikram Yoga, or Choudhury Yoga
A form of Hatha Yoga, which is also known as Hot Yoga. With a surrounding temperature of 100°F (38°C) or more, the yoga instructor leads the students through 26 postures that are designed to stretch muscles and tendons in a specific order. The heat warms the muscles, and enables them to stretch farther.

Brahma
Major Hindu deity; the creator.

Brahman
The supreme reality according to Hinduism; conceived of as one; the ultimate principle underlying the world; ultimate reality.

Chakras
Various centers of energy in the human body, according to Hinduism or other Asian traditions. Some are located along the spine, and others along the horizontal center of the body. There are supposed to be seven basic chakras, which are found in different areas of the body and have different functions. The

New Age movement has also adopted the chakras and their application.

Choudhury Yoga
See Bikram Yoga

Cobra pose
A posture of Hatha Yoga, where a person resembles a cobra with its head raised.

Corpse pose, or Savasana
A relaxing posture, which is often used to begin or conclude a yoga session. In this posture the person lies with his back on the floor as if "dead."

Dharana
A spiritual exercise of Hinduism. It consists of deep concentration or mind control. It is also called a centering technique that is supposed to lead one to experience the divine within oneself.

Dharmakaya
Means 'reality body' and is understood to embody the very principle of enlightenment. It is part of the Trikaya doctrine, which is a Buddhist teaching both on the nature of reality and who Buddha is.

Dhyana

Described in Hindu thought as the awakening of awareness that is supposed to occur when one's attention is concentrated at one point, e.g. through contemplation or meditation.

Guru

In Hinduism, a spiritual teacher or guide who has attained spiritual insight, and who instructs the student in the use of a *mantra*, to assist him with his personal meditation.[45]

Hatha Yoga
A branch of Raja Yoga that emphasizes physical postures and breathing techniques.

Ishvar, or Ishwar
A Hindu philosophical concept of god, meaning that entity or the supreme being which is the lord and the ruler of everything.

Iyengar Yoga
A form of Hatha Yoga that is often used as the beginner yoga. Iyengar focuses on aligning the body to help students who lack flexibility. It is used for physical therapy because its focus on the movement of the joints.

Jivamukti Yoga
A variation of Ashtanga Yoga with a focus on spiritual training that includes chanting, meditation, and readings.

Jnana Yoga

One of the four major yogic paths of Hinduism. It emphasizes knowledge and wisdom. Through strength of will and intellect, the yogi attempts to remove the barriers to his unity with the spirit.

Karma

Described in Hinduism as the universal law by which a person's actions determine his future mode of existence. The concept of *karma* is closely interwoven with *samsara* and *moksha*.[46]

Karma Yoga

One of the four major paths of yoga in Hinduism. It is action oriented and emphasizes the purification of the heart to act selflessly, and detaching ourselves from thinking about the fruits of our actions.

Katha Upanishad

One of the older, "primary" Upanishads. It consists of a dialogue concerning life after death between a devotee named Naciketa and the ruler of death. It is also known for introducing the term yoga with reference to spiritual exercise.

Kripalu Yoga

A form of Hatha Yoga that is also called the

yoga of consciousness. It teaches students to pay attention to their physical and psychological reaction to different postures. Three stages are involved: learning the postures, holding the postures, and combining them into a kind of meditation in motion.

Kundalini
The so-called serpent power that is believed to be located at the base of the human spine. In the normal state it is believed to be asleep; through yoga or meditation it can be awakened and will rise through the *chakras* (channels of energy) and ultimately to the brain.

Kundalini Shakti
Shakti stands for the underlying energy of life and often represents feminine energy derived from the female part of god, which in Hinduism is called "The Divine Mother" or "Mother Earth." In yoga, *Kundalini Shakti* is also called serpent power and represents the life energy that is supposed to be curled up like a snake at the base of the human spine.

Kudalini Yoga
Also called the yoga of awareness. It emphasizes chanting, meditation, physical postures, and breathing techniques.

Lotus position

A sitting position in yoga with crossed legs, in which each foot, with sole upturned, rests on the thigh of the opposing leg.[47]

Mahabarata

One of India's two great epic poems, the other being the *Ramayana*. It is the longest epic work in the world, eight times the length of Homer's *Iliad* and *Odyssey* combined. It describes the struggle and civil war between the Kauravas and the Pandavas (two groups of people). The *Bhagavad-Gita* is also part of the *Mahabarata*.

Mantra

A religious/sacred utterance that is recited during meditation or prayer. *Mantras* can be spoken out loud or just be recited in one's thoughts. If they are repeated it is called "chanting." They are believed to have mystical power and are supposed to help a devotee achieve singular focus.

Medium

A person who is able to make contact with the worlds of spirits, especially while being in a state of trance.[48]

Moksha

Liberation from the cycle of death and rebirth (*samsara*). It literally means the freedom from *samsara*. This concept of liberation is shared by religions like Hinduism, Buddhism, and Jainism.[49]

Nirvana

A Buddhist concept of a final state of being when human beings are no longer impacted by external things. This state transcends suffering and is believed to be reached through the extinction of desire and individual consciousness.[50]

Niyama

Rules of conduct that are found in numerous Hindu scriptures including the *Yoga Sutras* by Patanjali. They are described as guidelines for the attitudes people should develop towards their "inner self."

Occult

Often described as supernatural beliefs, practices, or phenomena which are mysterious, secret, concealed, or hidden from view; also described as being beyond common knowledge or experience or even as esoteric.

Prajna

Wisdom that is believed to bring about enlightenment; also considered a means to reach *nirvana*.

Pranayama

A breathing exercise that involves breath control through certain techniques. It aims to lead a person to a state of perfect concentration, where the focus on bodily functions is not present anymore.[51]

Pratyahara
Withdrawal of the senses from attachment to external objects or outward stimulants. It is described as a state of internal concentration where one's senses are no longer influenced by outward things.

Psychotropic drugs
Drugs which are capable of affecting the mind, emotions, and behavior.[52]

Purusa, or Purusha
According to Hindu thought, the eternal, unchanging self.

Raja Yoga
One of the four major yogic paths of Hinduism. It is the science of physical and mental control, and focuses on methods to control thoughts by turning mental and physical energy into spiritual energy.

Ramayana
The second great epic poem of India, besides the *Mahabarata*. It describes the love story of an

ancient king, Rama, and his wife Sita through allegory in narrative and through the interspersion of the philosophical and devotional.

Reincarnation
The belief that the soul is reborn in one or more successive instances in another form, either as a human being or animal or in some instances as a plant.[53]

Samadhi
Described in Hindu philosophy as the highest state of mental concentration that a human being can achieve while still bound to this body. The achievement of this state of concentration is believed to unite a human being with the highest reality (*Brahman*).[54]

Samsara
Described in Indian philosophy as the concept of the soul trying to find release from the bonds of its past deeds (*karma*).[55]

Serpent Power
See *kundalini*

Shamanism
A complex pattern of diverse rites and beliefs concerning the communication with the spirit world. A practitioner of Shamanism is called a

shaman. Shamans see themselves as intermediaries between humans and the spirit world. When a Shaman is initiated, it typically involves a visionary death or a trancelike out-of-body experience. By returning from death a Shaman is believed to attain secret power to influence the spirit world.[56]

Sivananda Yoga
A form of Hatha Yoga that calls for the rigorous application of yoga postures, breathing exercises, relaxation, vegetarian diet. It also involves the study of Hindu scriptures.

Sushumna, or Shushumna
Described in yoga as the body's main energy channel, which connects the base *chakra* at the center of the spine with the crown *chakra* of the head. It is also described as the channel through which the awakened *kundalini* flows.

Sutra
An aphorism in Hinduism like a rule or a guideline in the form of a short sentence to recall or cite Hindu philosophical texts.

Transcendental Meditation
A method of meditation based on such Hindu techniques as frequent repetition of a personal *mantra*.[57]

Upanishads
A collection of speculative treatises which primarily discuss meditation and philosophy.

Vedas
Ancient writings that form an integral part of the foundation of Hinduism.

Vedic Astrology, or Jyotish
A system based on star time and positions which are believed to associate people's inner qualities and paths in life with their times and places of birth.[58]

Vendantic philosophy
A school of philosophy based on the Vedas and focused on trying to understand the nature of reality.

Viniyoga
A form of Hatha Yoga. It is the most highly customized form of yoga. The stretching postures are adjusted to each student's needs and abilities. The function of a posture is emphasized over its form, with a focus on integrating the flow of breath with the movement of the spine.

Yama
The first of the eight limbs of Raja Yoga according to Patanjali. It is seen as a kind of

codex of behavior that emphasizes restraint and self control.

Yoga Sutras

A classical text from the yoga school of Indian philosophy that is the foundation of all yoga systems and was written by Patanjali between 300 and 500 A.D.

Yogi

In general, one who practices yoga. However, normally the term *yogi* is reserved for more advanced practitioners of yoga.

Notes

[1] "Yoga in America Market Study." Yoga Journal, 26 Feb. 2008, 03 Aug. 2009 <http://www.yogajournal.com/advertise/press_rele ases/10>.

[2] John Ankerberg and John Weldon, Encyclopedia of New Age Beliefs. (Eugene, OR: Harvest House, 1996) 601.

[3] Robert A.F. Thurman, "Reality Check: Renowned Buddhist scholar Robert Thurman reflects on the Yoga Sutra and how we can know reality for ourselves." Yoga Journal, March/April 2001: 70.

[4] Louis Hughes. Yoga - A Path to God? (Dublin, Ireland: Mercier, 1997) 21.

[5] "Yoga in America Market Study." Yoga Journal, 26 Feb. 2008, 03 Aug. 2009 <http://www.yogajournal.com/advertise/press_rele ases/10>.

[6] Yoga Today: 100 Years of Yoga in America, videocassette, Unity in Yoga, 1993.

7 "A shopper's guide," Time Magazine U.S. Edition, 23 Apr. 2001: 63.

8 "Yoga Postures," Holistic online.com, n.d., 02 Jul. 2002 <http://www.holistic-online.com/Yoga/hol_yoga_pos_intro.htm#introduction>.

9 Ravi Ravindra, "Yoga and the Quintessential Search for Holiness." Journal of Dharma, 1995: 249.

10 Ravindra 250.

11 Thomas Matus, "Yoga, Multi-Culturalism, and Evangelization." Studia Missionalia, 1995: 257.

12 Jakob W. Hauer, "Ist der Yoga ein Weg zum Heil." Kairos, 1961: 193.

13 Brad Scott, "The Watchman Expositor: Yoga: Exercise or Religion?" Watchman Fellowship, 2001, 15 Jul. 2002 <http://www.watchman.org/na/yogareligion.htm>.

14 Johanna Michaelsen, Like Lambs to the Slaughter. (Eugene, OR: Harvest House, 1977) 93-95.

15 Irving Hexham quoted in, Ruth A. Tucker, Another Gospel. (Grand Rapids, MI: Academie) 387.

[16] Tara's story as told to Armin Weidle in Oct. 2005.

[17] Ankerberg and Weldon 596.

[18] "Yoga - Relaxation or Occult?" <u>Biblical Discernment Ministries</u>, Jan. 2002, 30 Jul. 2002 <http://www.rapidnet.com/~jbeard/bdm/Psychology/yoga.htm>.

[19] Donald J. DeGracia, "CSP – Psychedelics/Kundalini Survey Results." <u>Council on Spiritual Practices</u>, 1995, 25 Jul. 2002 <http://www.csp.org/practices/entheogens/docs/kundalini_survey.html>.

[20] <u>Yoga Today: 100 Years of Yoga in America</u>, videocassette, Unity in Yoga, 1993.

[21] Tony Quinn quoted in Hughes 35.

[22] Diane Barnes, Phone interview, Jun. 2002.

[23] Dave Hunt and T.A. McMahon, <u>The Seduction of Christianity</u>. (Eugene, OR: Harvest House, 1985) 89.

[24] Hunt and McMahon 54.

[25] Maharishi Mahesh quoted in Sarah E. Pavlik "Is Yoga really so bad?" <u>Christianity Today International/Today's Christian Woman Magazine</u>, 2001: 50.

[26] Ravindra, p. 251.

[27] Sri Swami Chidananda. "Yoga and Christianity."
The Divine Life Society, 17 Oct. 2004, 20 Jul. 2005.
<http://www.sivanandadlshq.org/religions/yogach
ristian.htm>.

[28] Sri Swami Chidananda. "Yoga and Christianity."
The Divine Life Society, 17 Oct. 2004, 20 Jul. 2005.
<http://www.sivanandadlshq.org/religions/yogach
ristian.htm>.

[29] "Occult." Webster's New World College Dictionary,
(New York: Macmillan, 1996) 937.

[30] Michaelsen 93-95.

[31] Ankerberg and Weldon 603.

[32] Gopi Krishna, Living with Kundalini: the
Autobiography of Gopi Krishna, (Boston, MA:.
Shambhala, 1993) 125.

[33] Krishna 126.

[34] Swami Narayanananda, quoted in Ankerberg and
Weldon 607.

[35] Rabindranath Maharaj, Death of a guru, (Eugene,
OR: Harvest House, 1984) 203.

[36] Mineda McCleave, quoted in Ankerberg and Weldon 608.

[37] Mineda McCleave, quoted in Ankerberg and Weldon 608.

[38] Marja Savola, "Kundalini & Liberating breathing or Rebirthing." <u>Kundalini Information & Kundalini Network</u>, 19 Nov. 2006, 12 Jul. 2007 <http://kundalini.se/eng/breath.html>.

[39] Jean-Marie Dechanet, quoted in Hughes 111.

[40] Hughes 165.

[41] Nancy Roth, <u>An Invitation to Christian Yoga</u>, (Cambridge, MA: Cowley, 2001) 6.

[42] Roth 87.

[43] Susan Bordenkircher, "Outstretched in Worship." <u>Christian Yoga</u>, n.d., 20 Mar. 2008 <http://www.christianyoga.us/instructor.htm>.

[44] Laurette Willis, "What A Class Looks Like." <u>PraiseMoves®</u>, n.d., 28 Jul. 2010. <http://praisemoves.com/about-us/what-a-class-looks-like/>.

[45] "Guru." <u>Encyclopædia Britannica Online</u>, 2009, 28

Jul. 2009
<http://www.britannica.com/EBchecked/topic/249
714/guru>.

46 "Karma." Encyclopædia Britannica Online, 2009, 26
Aug. 2009
<http://www.britannica.com/EBchecked/topic/312
474/karma>.

47 "Lotus position." LoveToKnow, n.d., 26 Aug. 2009
<www.yourdictionary.com/lotus-position>.

48 "Medium." Encyclopædia Britannica Online, 2009,
28 Jul. 2009
<http://www.britannica.com/EBchecked/topic/372
730/medium>.

49 "Moksha" Encyclopædia Britannica Online, 2009, 26
Aug. 2009
<http://www.britannica.com/EBchecked/topic/387
852/moksha>.

50 "Nirvana." Encyclopædia Britannica Online, 2009,
29 Aug. 2009
<http://www.britannica.com/EBchecked/topic/415
925/nirvana>.

51 "Prāāyāma." Encyclopædia Britannica Online, 2009,
27 Aug. 2009
<http://www.britannica.com/EBchecked/topic/473
945/pranayama>.

52 "Psychotropic drug." <u>MedicineNet</u>, 17 Feb. 2004, 24 Jul. 2009 <http://www.medterms.com/script/main/art.asp?a rticlekey=30807>.

53 "Reincarnation." <u>Encyclopædia Britannica Online</u>, 2009, 26 Aug. 2009 <http://www.britannica.com/EBchecked/topic/496 541/reincarnation>.

54 "Samadhi." <u>Encyclopædia Britannica Online</u>, 2009, 26 Aug. 2009 <http://www.britannica.com/eb/article-9065178>.

55 "Samsara." <u>Encyclopædia Britannica Online</u>, 2009, 26 Aug. 2009 <http://www.britannica.com/EBchecked/topic/520 716/samsara>.

56 "Shamanism." <u>Encyclopedia of Alternative Medicine</u>. The Gale Group Inc., 2005, 27 Jul. 2009 <http://www.answers.com/topic/shamanism>.

57 "Transcendental Meditation." <u>LoveToKnow</u>, n.d., 24 Jul. 2009 <http://<www.yourdictionary.com/transcendental-meditation>.

58 "Vedic astrology." <u>knowledgerush.com</u>, 15 Jul. 2009, 23 Jul. 2009

<http://www.knowledgerush.com/kr/encyclopedia
/Vedic_astrology/>.

Armin Weidle

Resources

Books And Articles:

Ankerberg, John, and John Weldon. Encyclopedia of New Age Beliefs. Eugene, OR: Harvest House, 1996.

"A shopper's guide." Time Magazine U.S. Edition 157.16 (2001): 63.

Foster, Richard J. Celebration of Discipline: the Path to Spiritual Growth. San Francisco: Harper & Row, 1988.

Hauer, Jakob W. "Ist der Yoga ein Weg zum Heil?" Kairos 3-4 (1961): 189-95.

Hexham, Irving. "Yoga, UFOs and Cult Membership." Update: A Quarterly Journal of New Religious Movements 10.3 (1986): 3-17.

Hughes, Louis. Yoga - A Path to God? Dublin, Ireland: Mercier, 1997.

Hunt, Dave, and T.A. McMahon. The Seduction of Christianity: Spiritual Discernment in the Last Days. Eugene, OR: Harvest House, 1985.

Krishna, Gopi. Living with Kundalini: the Autobiography of Gopi Krishna. Boston, MA: Shambhala, 1993.

Levinson, David, and Laura Gaccione. Health and Illness: A Cross-Cultural Encyclopedia. Santa Barbara, CA: ABC-CLIO, 1997.

Matus, Thomas. "Yoga, Multi-Culturalism, and Evangelization." *Studia Missionalia* 44 (1995): 251-74.

Michaelsen, Johanna. Like Lambs to the Slaughter. Eugene, OR: Harvest House, 1977.

Neufeldt, Victoria, and David B. Guralnik. Webster's New World College Dictionary. New York: Macmillan, 1996.

Pavlik, Sarah E. "Is Yoga really so bad?" Christianity Today International/Today's Christian Woman Magazine 23.5 (2001): 50.

Pflueger, Lloyd. Discriminating the innate Capacity: Salvation and Mysticism of classical Samkha-Yoga. New York, NY: The New York, Oxford University Press, 1998.

Ravindra, Ravi. "Yoga and the Quintessential Search for Holiness." Journal of Dharma 20.3 (1995):

245-53.

Rice, Edward. Eastern Definitions. Garden City, NY: Anchor, 1980.

Roth, Nancy. An Invitation to Christian Yoga. Cambridge, MA: Cowley, 2001.

Sin, Jack. Examining and exposing Cultic and Occultic movements. Singapore: Marantha Bible Presbyterian Church, 2000.

Sorge, Bob. Secrets of the Secret Place. Lee's Summit, MO: Oasis House, 2001.

Thurman, Robert A. F. "Reality Check: Renowned Buddhist scholar Robert Thurman reflects on the Yoga Sutra and how we can know reality for ourselves." Yoga Journal March/April (2001): 67-71.

Tucker, Ruth A. Another Gospel: Alternative Religions and the New Age Movement. Grand Rapids, MI: Academie Books, 1989.

Watson, William G. A Concise Dictionary of Cults & Religions. Chicago: Moody, 1991.

White, John. Kundalini Evolution and Enlightment. Garden City, NY: Anchor, 1979.

Videos:

Yoga Today: 100 Years of Yoga in America.
Lakewood, CO: Unity in Yoga, 1993.

Websites:

Bordenkircher, Susan. "Outstretched in Worship."
Christian Yoga. n.d. Web. 20 Mar. 2008.
<http://www.christianyoga.us/instructor.htm
>.

Chidananda, Sri Swami. "Yoga and Christianity." The
Divine Life Society. 17 Oct. 2004. Web. 20 Jul.
2005.
<http://www.sivanandadlshq.org/religions/
yogachristian.htm>.

DeGracia, Donald J. "CSP – Psychedelics/Kundalini
Survey Results." Council on Spiritual Practices,
1995. Web. 25 Jul. 2002.
<http://www.csp.org/practices/entheogens/
docs/kundalini_survey.html>.

"Encyclopedia Britannica Online." Encyclopedia
Britannica Inc., 2009. Web. Jul./Aug. 2009.
<http://www.britannica.com/>.

"Encyclopedia of Alternative Medicine." The Gale
Group Inc., 2005. Web. 27 Jul. 2009.
<http://www.answers.com/topic/shamanism

>.

Gleghorn, Michael. "Yoga and Christianity: Are They Compatible?" Probe Ministries, 2002. Web. 20 Jul. 2002. <http://www.probe.org/site/c.fdKEIMNsEo G/b.4217629/k.15B5/ Yoga_and_Christianity_Are_They_Compatible .htm>.

"Knowledgerush Encyclopedia." Knowledgerush.com, 2009. Web. 23 Jul. 2009. <http://www.knowledgerush.com/kr/enyclo pedia/Main_Page/>.

Savola, Marja. "Kundalini & Liberating breathing or Rebirthing." Kundalini Information & Kundalini Network, 19 Nov. 2006. Web. 12 Jul. 2007. <http://kundalini.se/eng/breath.html>.

Scott, Brad. "The Watchman Expositor: Yoga - Exercise or Religion?" Watchman Fellowship, 2001. Web. 15 Jul. 2002. <http://www.watchman.org/na/yogareligion .htm>.

"MedTerms™ Medical Dictionary." MedicineNet, 2009. Web. 24 Jul. 2009. <http://www.medterms.com/script/main/hp .asp>.

Montenegro, Marcia. "Yoga: Yokes, Snakes, and Gods." 23 Sept. 2004. Web. 20 Jan. 2007. <http://cana.userworld.com/cana_yoga.html>.

Valea, Ernest. "Possible difficulties in Yoga as a spiritual path towards transcendence." Comparative Religion, 16 Jun. 2010. Web. 10 Jul. 2010. <http://www.comparativeligion.com/Yoga.html>.

Willis, Laurette. "What A Class Looks Like." PraiseMoves®, n.d. Web. 28 Jul. 2010. <http://www.praisemoves.com/about-us/what-a-class-looks-like/>.

"Yoga - Relaxation or Occult?" Biblical Discernment Ministries, Jan. 2002. Web. 30 Jul. 2002. <http://www.rapidnet.com/~jbeard/bdm/Psychology/yoga.htm>.

"Yoga." Erowid Yoga Vault, 08 Jul. 2006. Web. 20 Jan 2007. <http://www.erowid.org/spirit/yoga/yoga.shtml>.

"Yoga-Geschichte." East-Side-Yoga, 2003. Web. 20 Jan. 2007. <http://www.east-side-yoga.de/html/geschichte.html>.

"Yoga in America Market Study." Yoga Journal, 26 Feb. 2008. Web. 03 Aug. 2009.
<http://www.yogajournal.com/advertise/press_releases/10>.

"Yoga Postures." Holisticonline.com, n.d. Web. 02 Jul. 2002.
<http://www.holistic-online.com/Yoga/hol_yoga_pos_intro.htm#introduction>.

"Your Dictionary.com." LoveToKnow, Corp., 2009. Web. 24 Jul. 2009.
<http://yourdictionary.com/>.

Phone Interviews:

Diane Barnes, "Mind-Body-Health," Columbia, SC: Jun. 2002.

Nicki Music, "Columbia Yoga Center," Columbia, SC: Jun. 2002.

About the Author

Born and raised in Germany, Armin Weidle also lived for almost five years in the U.S., where he earned a degree in Biblical Studies and a Master of Arts in Intercultural Studies. He also spent time studying Indian culture, both in the U.S. and while living in India for some time. He is especially interested in helping people understand truth and shedding light on things that are hidden. *Bowing to Yoga?* is his first book. Today Armin works in business and lives near Frankfurt, Germany, with his wife Ratna and his three children.

Made in the USA
Columbia, SC
31 January 2022

54795414R00067